LONDON HOTELS

By Harry Palmer

SHANE
BOOKS

First published in 2022 by

Shane Books,
Flat 1, No. 21 The Ridgeway,
Enfield,
Middlesex. EN2 8NX

ISBN 978-1-9160230-0-0

CONTENTS

The Baglioni Hotel on the corner of De Vere Gardens was formerly the De Vere Hotel. The original name of the hotel derived from Aubrey de Vere, the first Lord of the Manor of Kensington.

Bailey's Hotel, Courtfield Gardens is now shorn of its original wrought iron entrance and flanking gas lamps.

Next to Gloucester Road Underground Station Bailey's Hotel was built during the 1870's.

The bar area of Bailey's Hotel.

Original planning for the Hotel was for eleven floors with 300 bedrooms on the nine upper floors. Contractors were Holloway Bros. (London) Ltd., Art Metal Work was by Jones & Willis Ltd., and Ironmongery was by Pfeil, Stedall & Co.

Above can be seen the Bonnington Hotel as it is today and below as it was in 1914. The Bonnington Hotel's architect was W. Ernest Hazell.

Edward Middleton Barry's hotel facade to the Strand has been altered by the addition of two upper storeys.

The Charing Cross Hotel's facade was one of the first facades in England to use reconstituted stone.

The Charing Cross Hotel's restaurant has superb views overlooking The Strand.

Above can be seen the side of Charing Cross Hotel with both Charing Cross Underground Station and Charing Cross Overground Station nearby.

Claridge's Hotel, 1895 - 1898, was built by Munt and Stephens.

The main reception rooms which were fitted out by Ernest George and Yeates and the entrance hall with staircase and ballroom remain.

The Connaught Hotel in Carlos Place, Mayfair dates from 1897 when the Coburg Hotel was re-opened.

In 1917 the name was changed to "Connaught" after Queen Victoria's third son the Duke of Connaught.

The Corinthea Hotel, originally the Metropole Hotel, was the base for the Aero Club and the Alpine Club and acted as the gathering point for competitors in the first London to Brighton run in 1896.

The Corinthea Hotel was originally built as the Metropole Hotel and construction started in 1883 and the hotel opened in 1885.

The Dorchester Hotel was designed in 1930 by W. Curtis Green.

Owen Williams designed the structure but resigned when there were objections to his plans for covering the frame.

The Goring Hotel dates from 1910.

The Goring Hotel is at the junction of Victoria Square and Beeston Place.

The Grosvenor House Hotel on Park Lane was built 1926 - 1928 by Wimperis, Simpson and Guthrie. Edwin Lutyens was consultant and designed only the elevations.

The hotels 478 bedrooms and 160 flats are contained in four closely packed blocks and although very large it does not have the height of the Royal Lancaster Hotel nor the London Hilton Hotel.

The Grosvenor Hotel, Buckingham Palace Road, was built in 1860 by J. T. Knowles.

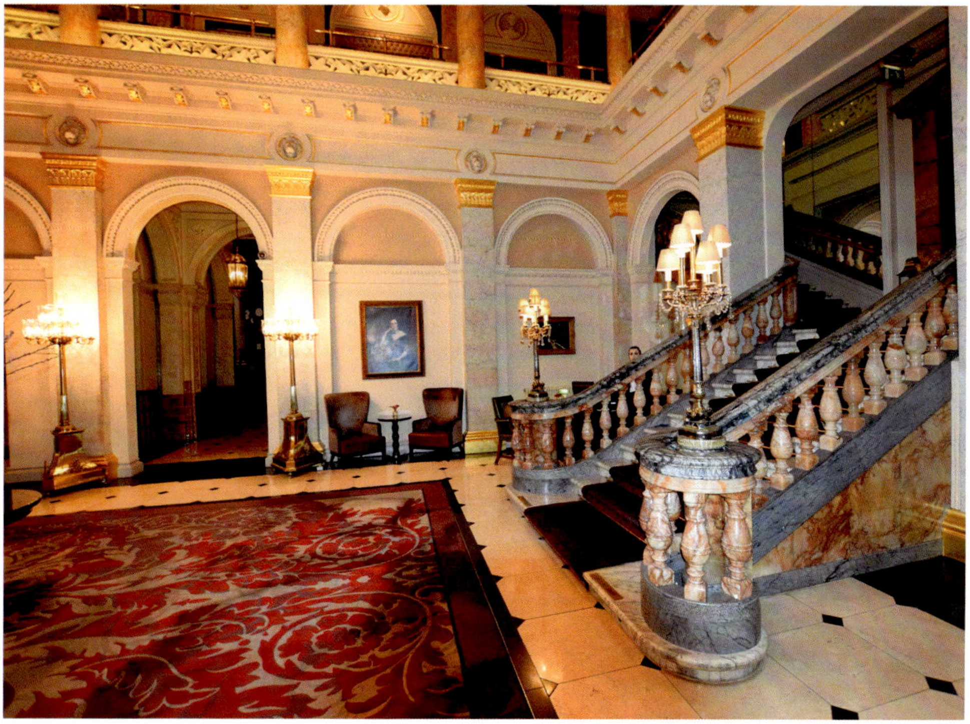

The Grosvenor Hotel, though not the first station hotel in London, was one of the first examples of the French 'Second Empire' style.

The large scale design of the Grosvenor Hotel, an elaborately decorated rectangle of brick and stone is typical of the railway age.

The Grosvenor Hotel has been described as one of the representative monuments of Victorian London.

This is the bar area of the Grosvenor Hotel.

On the first and top storeys, between the arched windows are portraits of Queen Victoria, Prince Albert and Lord Palmerston.

The Hotel Café Royal is at 66 Regent Street and is a grade II listed building.

Patrons have included Oscar Wilde, Virginia Woolf, D. H. Lawrence and George Bernard Shaw.

The Inter-Continental Hotel at 1 Hamilton Place on Hyde Park Corner and Park Lane was opened by His Grace the 8th Duke of Wellington on 23rd September 1975. It stands on the very site of what was 145 Piccadilly, the Queen's former childhood residence.

The Inter-Continental Hotel underwent a £75 million pound refurbishment in 2007.

The Inter-Continental Hotel was designed by British architect Sir Frederick Gibberd whose other notable designs included the Liverpool Metropolitan Cathedral and the London Central Mosque in Regent's Park.

The Kensington Forum Hotel is located at 97 Cromwell Road.

The Langham Hotel opened on the 10th June 1865.

The Langham Hotel was designed by John Giles and built between 1863 and 1865.

The Langham Hotel is in the district of Marylebone at 1c Portland Place. Sir Arthur Conan Doyle was a frequent hotel guest.

In 1871 Louis Napoleon III spent much of his enforced exile from France at The Langham, London.

The Landmark London, at 222 Marylebone Road, was designed by architect Colonel Sir Robert William Edis.

The Landmark Hotel London dates back to 1899 and was originally opened by the Great Central Railway as the Hotel Great Central.

The Landmark Hotel served as the headquarters of the British Railway Board before reopening as a hotel in 1993.

It was John Blundell Maple (of the furniture company Maples) who opened his hotel here in 1899.

St. Georges Hospital had been established on the site of the current Lanesborough Hotel in 1733 in a Country home built in 1719 by James Lane, 2nd Viscount Lanesborough.

In 1826 the trustees of St. Georges commissioned William Wilkins to design a new hospital. Wilkins was also the architect for the National Gallery in Trafalgar Square.

The building was subject to a four year restoration project from 1988 to 1991.

The facade to Hyde Park Corner of the Lanesborough Hotel has a central porch of square columns, with two side wings divided into two bays by a central pilaster.

The hospital was enlarged in the mid-nineteenth century but eventually closed in 1980. Redeveloped as a hotel Wilkin's facades were restored.

The London Hilton Hotel on Park Lane was designed by Lewis Soloman Kaye and built in 1963 and marked the arrival of 'Manhattanism'.

The Mandarin Oriental Hyde Park is opposite the Harvey Nichols department store at 66 Knightsbridge.

The Mandarin Oriental Hotel originally opened as the Hyde Park Hotel in 1902. Today the hotel contains 198 rooms and suites.

Three union-jack flags over the entrance to the May Fair Hotel can be seen above.

The May Fair Hotel, Stratton Street, is the official hotel for London Fashion Week.

The Milestone Hotel, 1 Kensington Court, has 44 guest bedrooms, 12 suites and 6 long-stay apartments.

The Milestone is a five-star, Grade II listed building.

The Millennium Gloucester Hotel is a four-star hotel with 610 rooms.

The Millennium Gloucester Hotel is located at 4-18 Harrington Gardens, Kensington.

Like Bailey's Hotel, the Millennium Gloucester Hotel is very close to Gloucester Road tube station.

The Millennium Hotel, Knightsbridge is located at 17 Sloane Street, Knightsbridge.

Now Le Meridien, the original Piccadilly hotel was designed by architect Richard Norman Shaw 1905-1908.

The Piccadilly Hotel was Shaw's last big building in his late heavy baroque style.

This is the Terrace restaurant of Le Meridien. The glazed restaurant on the terrace is a later addition.

The Queen's Hotel, Queens House, Leicester Square opened in 1899. In May 2012 the upper floors once again returned to hotel use when it was purchased for The Premier Inn.

THE QUEEN'S HOTEL.

LEICESTER SQUARE, LONDON.

MESSRS. SAVILLE & MARTIN, MM.S.A., ARCHITECTS.

THIS imposing building, erected on the north side of Leicester Square, occupies the entire frontage from the Empire Theatre to Leicester Place, and certainly constitutes one of the most important of the many recent improvements of this neighbourhood. It is a handsome and lofty structure of Portland stone and polished granite, executed in the style of the French Renaissance from the designs of Messrs. Saville & Martin.

The front part of the ground storey, it should be noted, projects beyond the main line of the building, and so provides room for a spacious terrace balcony, which, in a building of this class, is certainly a most pleasing and valuable feature.

Noble three-storied bay windows in the front gables contribute largely to the architectural effect of the front, and afford a view which will doubtless be appreciated by the visitors.

The central entrance is of a commanding character, and well deserves more than a casual examination. Carving and sculpture which embellish the exterior show an admirable variety and delicacy of detail.

From the point of view of public safety, it is satisfactory to state that the construction is of fireproof material throughout, there being not a particle of inflammable substance even in the partitions, staircases, or roofs. Notwithstanding this, none of the ordinary precautions have been omitted, and a complete system of hydrants has been provided on every floor.

There is also a good service of hydraulic elevators and service lifts, and the scheme of warming, ventilation, electric light, bells and telephones is very complete.

The front part of the ground floor is appropriated principally to the buffet, and beyond this is placed the grand dining hall, which is illustrated here.

Marble pilasters, paintings on ceilings and walls, electric lustres, and the onyx balustrading to the musicians' gallery give distinction to what must be admitted one of the finest banqueting chambers in the metropolis.

Downstairs the grill room almost rivals the grand dining-hall.

The front rooms on the first floor opening on to the balcony comprise drawing, reading and coffee rooms, and are large and well proportioned, being decorated in the Louis XV., Empire, and Louis XVI. styles respectively. A magnificent suite of masonic rooms are also on this floor. In addition, the building contains nearly a hundred bedrooms and private sitting rooms.

It is obvious that no amount of thought or expense has been spared on the sanitary arrangements, whilst the architects, in planning the building, have been particularly successful in securing an abundance of daylight throughout and the greatest facility of communication between the several parts.

The building was carried out by Messrs. Patman & Fotheringham, the general contractors.

The following Firms are amongst the principal Sub-Contractors who carried out important work in this Building:—

Steelwork.
Messrs. Homan & Rodgers.

Stonework.
Messrs. Webber & Corben.

Lifts.
The Otis Elevator Co., Ltd., 4, Queen Victoria Street, E.C. (see page 75).

Carving.
Mr. Halson.
Mr. Mabey.

Heating.
Messrs. Strode & Co., Ltd.

Electric Light.
Messrs. Wells, Rayner & Co., Ltd.

Granite, &c.
Messrs. Fenning & Co., Ltd.

Fire Escape Appliances.
Messrs. Merryweather & Co., Ltd.

Hot Water Engineers.
Messrs. Haden & Sons.

Ironmongery.
Messrs. C. & F. Smith.

QUEEN'S HOTEL, LEICESTER SQUARE.

BUILDERS: MESSRS. PATMAN & FOTHERINGHAM, LTD. ARCHITECTS: MESSRS. SAVILLE & MARTIN, MM.S.A.

The Queen's Hotel, Leicester Square as it is today.

The Ritz Hotel was built in 1906 and designed by Mewés and Davis who also designed the Royal Automobile Club, Pall Mall.

The Ritz seen above in 1914 before the motor car and below as it is today.

THE RITZ HOTEL,

PICCADILLY, LONDON, W.

MESSRS. MEWÈS & DAVIS, AND JOHN P. BISHOP, A.R.I.B.A., ARCHITECTS.

THIS hotel, built on the American steel frame system, stands on the site of a large block of offices known as Walsingham House, and was the first complete example in this country of the American method of construction. It has a frontage to Piccadilly of 230 feet, to Arlington Street of 115 feet, and to the Green Park of 87 feet, the cubical contents being 2,413,000 feet. Up to the first floor level the front walls are of Norwegian grey granite, and above that of Portland stone with brick backing.

The ground floor comprises the entrance hall, grand gallery, staircase, offices, restaurant, dining room, and Winter garden, while the upper floors are devoted to suites of rooms. There are over 150 bedrooms and 75 bathrooms. Partitions and floors throughout the hotel are of fireproof construction, and the glazing is fire-resisting.

Practically the whole of the decoration is carried out in Louis XVI. style, and executed by Messrs. Waring & Gillow, an outstanding feature being the two life-size figures at entrance to restaurant in bronze vert, holding gilded bronze lustres and mounted on pedestals of Echaillon stone. This stone also enters into the decoration of the Winter garden, being used in the facing of the walls and for the fountain.

Ventilation is obtained by means of a cased fan driven by two 25 h.p. electric motors, which is capable of dealing with a million cubic feet of air per hour. This air is thoroughly washed and filtered before being driven into the building, and the inlets and extracts are so arranged that neither noise nor draught are noticeable. Two main intake tanks, from which lift and force pumps deal with 80,000 gallons every twelve hours, give a plentiful supply of water to all parts, and the hot-water service is obtained by steam-heated calorifiers capable of supplying 6,000 gallons of boiling water per hour.

On all floors a complete system of fire services, hydrants and extinguishers is installed. The kitchens and dependencies are all on the lower ground floor.

THE RITZ HOTEL—A BATHROOM.

THE RITZ HOTEL—STEEL CONSTRUCTION.

The Ritz Hotel was the first steel-framed building in London.

The Royal Lancaster Hotel on Lancaster Terrace opened in 1967.

The tower of the Royal Lancaster Hotel was designed by architect Richard Seifert.

The Royal Lancaster Hotel is situated very near to Lancaster Gate Underground Station.

Architect Richard Seifert also designed Tower 42 and Centrepoint Tower.

The Russell Hotel was built in 1898 to the designs of C. Fitzroy Doll.

The construction of The Russell Hotel was the first large incursion into Georgian Bloomsbury.

The Savoy Hotel was built 1889 and 1903-1904 by A. H. Mackmurdo and Thomas Collcutt. The Savoy has two parts with that to the Strand by Thomas Collcutt and the bedroom wing facing the Thames by A. H. Mackmurdo.

In 1929 The Savoy's entrance court was restyled by Easton and Robertson, gaining the art deco stainless steel fascia.

In the Savoy Hotel some of Basil Ionide's interiors survive.

Bedroom wing facing the Thames is by Mackmurdo.

Only since 2016 has the hotel been known as the Sheraton Grand London Park Lane and it is a Grade II listed building with 303 bedrooms.

Above is the rear entrance to the Sheraton Grand Hotel. It was designed by architects Adie, Button and Partners in a grand Art Deco style.

The hotel was originally established by William Waldorf Astor 1st Viscount Astor.

Architect of The Waldorf Hotel was Marshall MacKenzie.

The Waldorf Hilton, London (formerly known as the Waldorf Hotel) is in Aldwych and has 298 guest rooms including 19 suites.

THE WALDORF HOTEL,

ALDWYCH, LONDON, W.C.

A. MARSHALL MACKENZIE, Esq., LL.D., F.R.I.B.A., & SON, Architects.

ON a conspicuous site in Aldwych the Waldorf Hotel is a striking and dignified architectural pile in this part of modern London. The facade to Aldwych is of Portland stone, upon a basement of Aberdeen granite, in Louis XVI. style. An effect of magnificence is obtained in the outlines, which are bold and simple, the only ornament being sculptured frieze capitals and vases. In the centre of the front is a screen in the Ionic style, correcting what might have appeared a monotonous array of regularly-placed windows.

The Waring-White Building Company completely finished, and Waring & Gillow furnished and equipped the building in about eighteen months—this rapid construction being possible by the method adopted, viz., steel skeleton with outer shell of stone. All floors and roofs are constructed of fire-proof materials. The grand lounge in the centre measures some 80 feet by 60 feet, and is surrounded by the public rooms of the hotel. There are some 400 bedrooms and over 150 bathrooms, several of the rooms being arranged in suites containing sitting, bed and bathrooms.

Ventilation of the grand lounge and grill room is obtained by means of two 15 in. double inlet fans, the fresh air before being distributed being filtered. All vitiated air is carried up a vertical shaft to the roof and extracted by a 40 in. fan.

Kitchen, scullery, stillroom and bakery are ventilated by a separate installation.

Low pressure steam radiators are used for the heating of the public rooms, corridors, and staircases, as are also the entrance halls. A main intake tank supplies the water, the tanks being situated in the basement, and the water being driven by electric pumps. They have a capacity of 24,000 gallons.

Mr. A. Marshall Mackenzie, the architect, has added to London another magnificent piece of architecture which is notable even among the other fine buildings which surround it.

The following Firms are amongst the principal Sub-Contractors who carried out important work in this Building :—

Electric Light Installation.
Aberdeen Electrical Engineering Co., Aberdeen.

Asphalte.
Messrs. Thos. Faldo & Co., Ltd., 1, Arundel Street, Strand.

Granolithic Stairs and Paving.
Stuart's Granolithic Co., Ltd., 4, Fenchurch Street.

Heating, Ventilating, Hot and Cold Water Services and Fire Hydrants.
Messrs. R. Crittall & Co., Ltd., 199, Wardour Street, W.

Passenger Lifts.
The Otis Elevator Co., Ltd., 4, Queen Victoria Street, E.C. (see page 75).

Service Lifts.
Messrs. Waygood & Co., Ltd., Falmouth Road, S.E. (see pages 104 and 175).

Plumbing and Sanitary Fittings.
Messrs. Shanks & Co., Ltd., 81, New Bond Street, W.

Joinery, Decoration and Furnishing.
Messrs. Waring & Gillow, Ltd., 180, Oxford Street, W.

Joinery.
Messrs. Samuel Elliott & Sons, Ltd., Caversham, Reading (see page 71).

Plastering.
Messrs. Henry Johnson & Sons, Ltd., Liverpool.

Slating.
Messrs. W. Allard & Co., Wandsworth Common.

Fire Escape Staircase.
St. Pancras Ironwork Co., Ltd., 171, St. Pancras Road, N.W. (see page 88).

Marble.
Messrs. Fenning & Co., Ltd., 3, Salter's Hall Court, E.C.

Reinforcing Bars.
Patented Indented Steel Bar Co., Ltd., Queen Anne's Chambers, Westminster (see page 25).

Fastening for Shop Window Glass.
Library Bureau, Ltd., 4, Cheapside, E.C.

Kitchen Fittings.
Messrs. Benham & Sons, Ltd.

Expanded Metal Reinforcements.
Expanded Metal Co., Ltd., York Mansions, York Street, S.W.

THE LOUNGE.

A BILLIARD ROOM.

WALDORF HOTEL.

STEEL CONSTRUCTION.

A pianist is a regular feature of the Waldorf Hotel.

The Wellesley, 11 Knightsbridge, is named after Sir Arthur Wellesley, the first Duke of Wellington and was originally one of the entrances to Hyde Park Corner tube station. Gibberd Architects were responsible for its reconstruction behind a retained facade of ox blood coloured tiles.

The Wellesley Hotel has 36 guest bedrooms and also houses the Crystal Bar and has a cigar terrace.